165 million years of
DINOSAURS

WRITER/PHOTOGRAPHER
François Gohier

SERIES EDITOR
Vicki León

DESIGNER
Ashala Nicols Lawler

SILVER BURDETT PRESS

© 1995 Silver Burdett Press
Published by Silver Burdett Press.
A Simon & Schuster Company
299 Jefferson Road, Parsippany, NJ 07054
Printed in the United States of America
10 9 8 7 6 5 4 3 2 1

CLOSE-UP
A Focus on Nature

SILVER BURDETT PRESS
© 1995 Silver Burdett Press
Published by Silver Burdett Press.
A Simon & Schuster Company
299 Jefferson Road, Parsippany, NJ 07054
Printed in the United States of America
10 9 8 7 6 5 4 3 2 1

Library of Congress
Cataloging-in-Publication Data
Gohier, François.
165 million years of dinosaurs: all about
theropods, sauropods, duck-billed dinosaurs, and a
T. rex or two/by François Gohier; photographs by
François Gohier.
    p. cm.--(Close up)
    ISBN 0-382-24903-8 (LSB)
    ISBN 0-382-24904-6 (SC)
    1. Dinosaurs--Juvenile literature.
[1. Dinosaurs.] I. Title. II. Series: Close up
(Parsippany, N.J.)
QE862.D5G677 1994
567.9'1--dc20   94-30912
                                   CIP
                                   AC

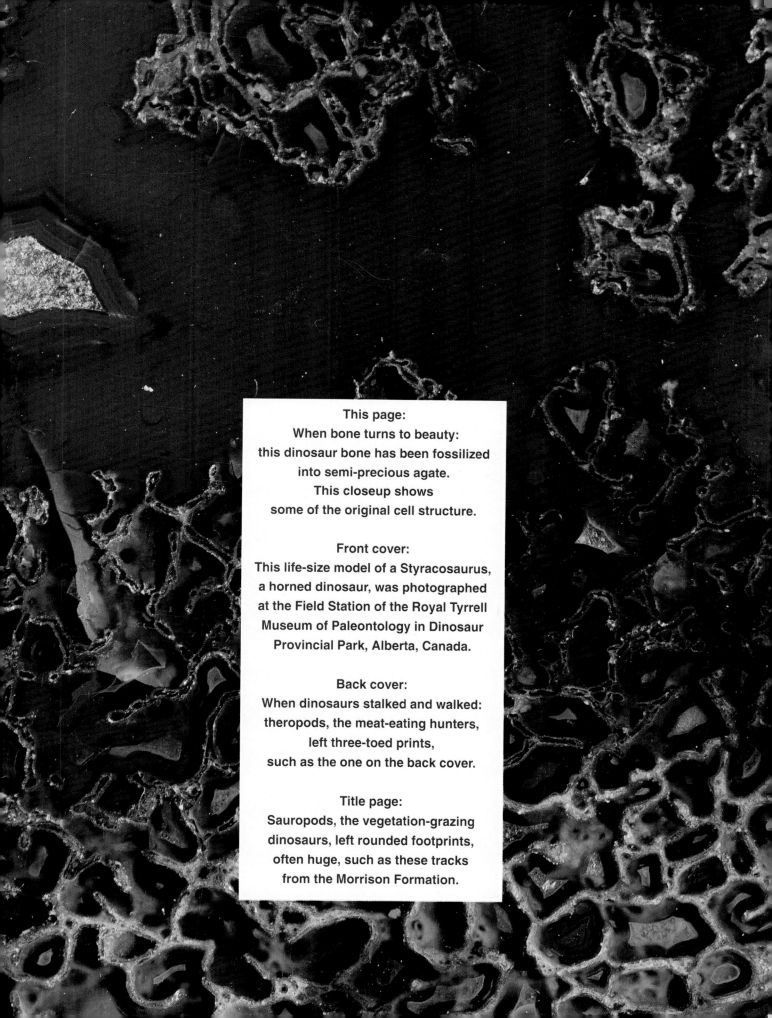

This page:
When bone turns to beauty:
this dinosaur bone has been fossilized
into semi-precious agate.
This closeup shows
some of the original cell structure.

Front cover:
This life-size model of a Styracosaurus,
a horned dinosaur, was photographed
at the Field Station of the Royal Tyrrell
Museum of Paleontology in Dinosaur
Provincial Park, Alberta, Canada.

Back cover:
When dinosaurs stalked and walked:
theropods, the meat-eating hunters,
left three-toed prints,
such as the one on the back cover.

Title page:
Sauropods, the vegetation-grazing
dinosaurs, left rounded footprints,
often huge, such as these tracks
from the Morrison Formation.

On the trail of
DINOSAURS

One hot Mexican afternoon, on an expedition with the Dinamation International Society, I was helping uncover the skeleton of a duck-billed dinosaur called a hadrosaur. Near our dig was a shallow pit. Fifteen years earlier, someone had excavated another hadrosaur from it.

As the afternoon light slid across the pit, a cry came from one of the workers.

"Mira!" he said. "Look!"

We all ran to look. On the floor of the pit we saw an imprint. It was the skin of a hadrosaur. Years ago, the dust and debris raised by that dig had hidden it. Now, cleaned by rain and wind, we saw the skinprint of an animal which had died and fallen on its side in the soft mud of a Cretaceous seashore, 70 million years ago.

That exciting find hooked me on dinosaur discoveries. As a naturalist, I've always been interested in large creatures, especially the whales. I've spent much of my life photographing humpbacks, grays, and orcas. It's no wonder I'm captivated by dinosaurs, who rivaled the whales in size and majesty.

For years, I've traveled to see the evidence left by dinosaurs. I work as a volunteer on digs. I visit trackways. I haunt museums, examining bones and gizzard stones. I interview experts and learn from paleontologists. In the process, my appreciation of dinosaurs grows and grows.

We live in the Golden Age of dinosaur discoverers and discoveries, and that's what this book is about. On some issues, the experts themselves don't agree. One thing we can be sure of: future finds are certain to change our picture of dinosaurs once again.

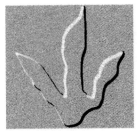

MORE THAN
'terrible reptiles'

WHAT SORT OF TEETH DID *T. REX* HAVE?

Photo, this page: big teeth with serrated edges, like steak knives. Most dinosaurs grew new teeth and replaced old ones all their lives.

People often use the word 'dinosaur' to describe something outdated. But 'dinosaur' could better be used to describe something that's vigorous, highly successful, and long-lived, with many diverse forms. Because that's exactly what dinosaurs as a group evolved to be.

Dinosaurs were a very special group of animals, like reptiles but different from all other reptiles and animals that have lived before or since. About 230 million years ago, they appeared on earth. Both meat-eating and plant-eating dinosaurs spread widely across our

planet, only to vanish about 65 million years ago. You might think of dinosaurs as 'unsuccessful,' since they became extinct. But they reigned supreme for 165 million years. That's a long run in anybody's terms!

What we know about dinosaurs comes mainly from discovering and studying their fossils. Fossils are remnants of animals or plants that have been buried after they died, quickly covered by sand or mud, and turned into rock. When rocks are eroded by time, fossils appear. Scientists call the study of fossils 'paleontology' – the study of great age.

How does a paleontologist know that a certain group of bones comes from a dinosaur and not from a reptile, like an alligator? A major difference lies in the shape of the hip socket and the position of the legs.

Look at a lizard or an alligator. Their legs spread away from the body. Now look at a bird. Its legs are vertical, supporting its body like two little pillars. The leg parts of most dinosaurs were built like bird's legs. The upper end of the thigh bone had a rounded head. It stuck out at nearly a 90-degree angle to join the hip bone. This arrangement made the leg go straight from the body to the ground. The dinosaur's weight sat directly on the vertical leg.

To tell dinosaurs from other fossil animals, scientists also look at details in the ankle and toe bones. All we need to remember is that dinosaurs walked erect.

Dinosaurs were first recognized as a distinct group in 19th-century England. For years, amateur and professional naturalists had found large bones and strange teeth in gravel pits and quarries of southern England. In 1825, a doctor named Gideon Mantell described teeth and other fragments of a large extinct reptile found by his wife Mary. He called it *Iguanodon*. To him, the teeth looked like those of a modern South American iguana. Today's iguana measures three- to four-feet long; Dr. Mantell's animal would have reached 30 feet or more.

Eventually it became obvious that these extinct creatures were different enough to warrant their own name. In 1841, Sir Richard Owen proposed the name 'dinosaur,' from the Greek meaning 'terrible reptile.'

The age of the dinosaurs covers most but not all of a huge geological era called the Mesozoic, or 'middle age of life,' on earth. The Mesozoic lasted about 179 million years. Scientists divide the Mesozoic into three smaller chunks called periods: the Triassic, the Jurassic, and the Cretaceous.

During this 179-million-year span, many things happened to our planet and the environments in which the dinosaurs lived. The climate changed. The continents moved. Mountains formed and disappeared. (These events continue today on earth.)

HOW BIG WAS TYRANNOSAURUS REX?
Ten-year-old James Smith, sitting near a cast of a T. rex skull at Smith Studios in Bozeman, Montana, helps us see.

5

At the beginning of the age of dinosaurs, the landmasses of the continents were connected in a supercontinent called Pangea. Because it was one landmass, the first dinosaurs were able to colonize most of the world.

When Pangea broke apart, the pieces slowly drifted towards their present-day positions. In the process, they carried along entire living

animal and plant communities. That's why we find dinosaur remains on all seven continents, including Antarctica. That's also a reason why some of the later species are only found in certain parts of the world. These dinosaurs evolved after the continents had begun to drift apart. Being land dwellers, they couldn't cross the seas.

Soon after their initial appearance, dinosaurs began to diversify. They became plant-eaters, meat-eaters or scavengers. They formed small, medium and large species.

The bigger dinosaurs were the largest animals to ever live on land. As a group, they dominated the landscape for many millions of years.

WHY ARE DINOSAURS CALLED 'BIRD-HIPPED' OR 'LIZARD-HIPPED'? Scientists divide them into two big groups, based on hipbone structure. They are either ornithischian ('bird-hipped') or saurischian ('lizard-hipped'). Tyrannosaurus rex, pictured opposite and on pages 2-3, was a lizard-hipped dinosaur.

Sometime near the beginning of the age of dinosaurs, the first mammals appeared. None got very big at this time. Why? Because any good-sized mammal in those days would have been mercilessly hunted or ambushed by the agile, two-legged dinosaur predators, such as *Velociraptor* or the big allosaurs. One of these small mammals was a distant – a very distant – ancestor of ours.

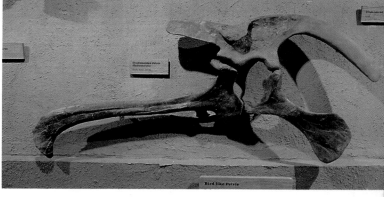

Many other animals lived during the same geological period. The strange flying reptiles, *Pteranodon* and its kind, were kin but not true dinosaurs. The huge marine reptiles, such as plesiosaurs and ichthyosaurs, were not dinosaurs, or even closely related. Land is where the dinosaurs thrived. No true dinosaur prospered in the seas or in the air.

At some point, a new type of creature appeared. We call them birds. The birds evolved from a small predatory dinosaur. In a way, then, dinosaurs are not totally extinct. Descended from one of the dinosaurs, this specialized group of beautiful feathered creatures is still with us today.

Scientists are often asked: Which animal is the largest to have ever lived on earth? As best we know, it's the blue whale. Whales live in the ocean, and only there. As far as land creatures, the largest were the four-legged, long-necked, plant-eating dinosaurs called sauropods.

Blue whales reach 100 feet. A really huge blue whale might weigh 180 tons. *Ultrasaurus* or *Brachiosaurus,* one of the biggest sauropods, may have been as long as 100 feet. A lot of its length was tail and neck. At 140 feet, *Seismosaurus* was the longest dinosaur we know of today. So the total body mass of even the biggest dinosaurs didn't come close to that of the blue whale.

Keep in mind that the name 'dinosaur' applies to an incredibly diverse collection of animals. Anatomy allows paleontologists to say that they form one group of animals. When we look at the photos in this book, we sometimes find it hard to see a family resemblance.

We also need to realize that during this long 'age of the dinosaurs,' many different species appeared, prospered, and then became extinct, giving rise to, or being replaced by, new species.

Scientists use many long words to describe dinosaur families. They divide them into two major groups: lizard-hipped (or saurischian) dinosaurs, and bird-hipped (or ornithischian) dinosaurs. The lizard-hipped group had both meat-eaters (theropods) and plant-eaters (sauropods).

The meat-eaters or predators walked on two legs. Most had three toes on each foot and a claw pointing back that barely touched the ground. Their footprints resemble bird footprints. Many species of theropods lived during the age of dinosaurs. The smallest predator was probably the size of a chicken. One of the biggest and most fearsome was *Tyrannosaurus rex.*

Then we come to the sauropods, the four-legged plant-eaters. These are the giants: *Diplodocus, Apatosaurus* (or *Brontosaurus*), *Supersaurus,* and *Brachiosaurus* among them. In North America, the sauropods flourished during the Jurassic period and then nearly disappeared. In Asia and South America, the sauropods survived until near the end of the Cretaceous.

VOLUNTEER
Dr. Lawrence Libecap, M.D.
takes part in a dinosaur dig,
sponsored by the
Dinamation International Society,
near Saltillo, Mexico.
Working with brushes
and other tools, Dr. Libecap helps
uncover a hadrosaur skeleton.

In contrast to the lizard-hipped group, all of the ornithischian or bird-hipped dinosaurs discovered to date were plant-eaters. Over 200 species have been found so far. They first appeared in the early Jurassic. Small dinosaurs like hypsilophodontids gave way to larger species, like the duck-billed dinosaurs.

The duck-billed dinosaurs or hadrosaurs and their relatives like *Iguanodon* were a large and successful group during the Cretaceous, well known for nesting in colonies and traveling in large herds. Most were bipedal, walking on two feet.

The armored and plated dinosaurs, such as nodosaurs, ankylosaurs, and stegosaurs, used protective armor. They had diverse defenses. Some had bony plates imbedded in the skin. Others possessed spikes that stuck out of their bodies to protect their sides.

One group, called the pachycephalosaurs, had thick caplike head-bones. They were related to the ceratopsids or horned dinos, which looked more like rhinos. They flourished in Cretaceous times. In the western part of North America, several spectacular species existed. You may know of *Triceratops*, which roamed Montana, Wyoming, and Alberta 65 to 70 million years ago. There was also a five-horned dinosaur called *Pentaceratops*, living in what is now New Mexico.

Both the horned dinosaurs and the duck-billed dinosaurs thrived until the final extinction of the dinosaurs.

TRIASSIC: birth of the dinosaurs

When the dinosaurs appeared, the world was not new. Life had been going on for hundreds of millions of years. Many strange animals lived on the land. There were mountains and volcanoes, plains and deserts, forests and lakes. There were beaches and storms, floods and sunny days. But for a very long time, something was missing: flowers. No roses, no apple trees, not even one small daisy.

Flowering plants came much later, many millions of years into the age of dinosaurs.

What did the plant-eating dinosaurs of that time live on? They ate ferns and conifers, such as pines. They also ate the early relatives of

the *Araucaria* or monkey-puzzle tree we now see in parts of South America and New Zealand. These trees reached an impressive size. You can get a good idea by visiting Arizona's Petrified Forest National Park. The logs, rocks, and fossils there date roughly from the beginning of the age of dinosaurs. Some of the earliest dinosaurs and mammals found to date came from this park.

Other important plants for hungry dinosaurs included relatives of the cycads. These are tough, palmlike plants that still grow in our tropics. Smaller plants, such as horsetails, fringed the ponds of the Triassic. These ancient species had already been on earth a long time before the dinosaurs showed up.

The first dinosaurs we know about walked on two legs. Small meat-eaters, these slender animals measured about six to ten feet long, with slim necks and tails. These early predators have been found in southern Brazil, in the foothills of the Argentinian Andes, and in the U.S. Paleontologists were able to find these dinosaurs because the rocks of that critical period, the late Triassic, are well preserved and exposed.

These little dinosaurs evolved from a group of reptiles which were also the forerunners of crocodiles. These animals, with names like *Eoraptor, Pisanosaurus,* and *Herrerasaurus,* had acquired the essential characteristic of dinosaurs: erect gait and body weight supported on straight legs. They were also the first animals to walk on two legs. Later, various species began to use four legs for locomotion. And so began the many different dynasties of dinosaurs.

Paleontologists have often wondered: Why were the dinosaurs so successful? Did they

MORRISON FORMATION

Running like a colorful stripe through the earth, the Morrison Formation winds from New Mexico into Alberta, Canada. In its layers, many great finds have been made: Brontosaurus (Apatosaurus); Diplodocus; Allosaurus; Stegosaurus; and more. Pictured is Dinosaur Hill, near Fruita, Colorado. Inset: gastroliths or 'gizzard stones,' used by some plant-eating dinosaurs to help digest food.

PALEONTOLOGIST
Ann Elder

studies the 200-foot quarry wall
rich with dinosaur bones
at Dinosaur National Monument
in Colorado. When not doing
field work, Ann spends time
in the DNM laboratory, pictured
opposite, to clean, identify,
and catalog her discoveries
and those of others.

possess some advantage that let them eliminate their competitors? After all, when dinosaurs came on the scene, the planet was well populated with a great variety of animals, including huge and dangerous reptiles. Did the dinosaurs compete with, and replace, the existing reptiles? Some say it had a lot to do with their athletic bipedal build and the large brains they developed to coordinate their improved movement.

Or was the dinosaurs' success due more to chance?

At the end of the Triassic period, a momentous event called a mass extinction took place. For reasons yet unknown to us, many species died out. Among those that survived were certain dinosaurs. Offered a new beginning, they flourished into a multitude of species. Nothing stopped them for many millions of years.

The mass extinction at the end of the Triassic is one of a series of similar events that have taken place throughout the history of the earth. The evolution of life has not followed a neat, orderly progression. Rather, at intervals, something totally unpredictable has occurred. At times, entire communities of well-adapted, successful animals have been wiped out, both on land and in the seas. These events were catastrophic. But they opened up new possibilities for the survivors.

JURASSIC: great age of dinosaurs

I f dinosaurs had written history books, they probably would have remembered the Jurassic as the most glorious period of their time on earth. In the Jurassic, dinosaurs evolved into many species, grew huge, and spread to live on all the continents.

Traces of the sauropods, the enormous plant-eaters of the Jurassic period, have been found in various parts of the world. In particular, many have come to light in western North America in the Morrison Formation. Running from New Mexico north and east into Utah, Colorado, Wyoming, and Alberta, Canada, the Morrison Formation is made up of layers of mudstone, in colorful shades of red or blue or gray, mixed with layers of hard sandstone that were once ancient stream channels. The great dinosaur skeletons that revolutionized American paleontology in the 19th century came from outcrops of the Morrison Formation.

The story begins about 1877. At that time, paleontologists Othniel C. Marsh of Yale University and Edward Drinker Cope from the Philadelphia Academy of Natural Science began their professional rivalry over dinosaur finds. Around this period, two teachers went fossil hunting in Colorado. Working independently, one found bones

near the little town of Morrison. He sent them to Cope, and later to Marsh. Marsh answered first. The other teacher prospected near Cañon City and shipped his finds to Cope. The Morrison Formation was beginning to yield its treasures.

More excitement occurred that same year at Como Bluff, west of Laramie, Wyoming. The managers of the Union Pacific Railroad found gigantic bones protruding from a hillside and notified Marsh. Their railroad cars provided the perfect means to send tons of fossils to the East Coast. Although Cope made the first drawing of a complete sauropod (the *Camarasaurus* from Colorado), Marsh used bones from Como Bluff to put together the first sauropod skeleton ever exhibited.

He called it *Brontosaurus* (also for technical reasons known as *Apatosaurus*). The term *Brontosaurus* is still such a household word that many people continue to use it.

Marsh and Cope competed for years, trying to outdo one another. Both excavated dozens of more or less complete skeletons from Wyoming, Colorado, New Mexico, and Montana. Between them, the two men named 130 different dinosaurs.

After Cope and Marsh died, one of the richest dinosaur quarries of all came to light in Utah in 1909. From it, Earl Douglass of the Carnegie Museum in Pittsburgh excavated large skeletons of *Diplodocus, Apatosaurus, Stegosaurus, Allosaurus,* and *Camarasaurus.* In 1915, this site became Dinosaur National Monument. Today it attracts half a million visitors each year, who marvel at the array of bones exposed on the steep face of a cliff.

Some 150 million years ago, the Morrison Formation was a broad plain, warm and periodically dry. There were ponds and lakes and some permanent rivers. There were large forests of tall conifer trees and cycad palms. Many species of dinosaurs lived there, including some of the most majestic animals to ever live on land. Largest of all were the sauropods, which moved slowly through the forests, reaching high into the trees to eat evergreen needles. Small-headed stegosaurs, their arched backs studded with triangular plates, ambled among the plants, perhaps even getting up onto their hind legs to eat the fronds of the cycads and tree-ferns. There were many species of small carnivorous dinosaurs, and *Allosaurus,* the most common carnivore, up to 35 feet long.

The large four-legged plant-eaters had small front teeth. They couldn't chew their food because they didn't have any molars. Instead, they swallowed vegetation and processed it later. Like modern birds, they had a gizzard, a special chamber where food is softened by muscle contractions before it is passed onto the stomach. Muscles aren't enough to do the trick. Again, like some birds, many of the big dinosaurs swallowed stones to help the process. When the stones became too small or smooth, they replaced them with larger ones.

How do we know this? The Morrison Formation has yielded many hard, perfectly polished stones, very different from the surrounding rocks. Some of these gastroliths or gizzard stones were found near or inside a dinosaur skeleton. In New Mexico, a *Seismosaurus* skeleton (possibly the longest of the sauropods) was found with several dozen gastrolith pebbles inside the rib cage of the animal. This exciting find was made by Dr. David Gillette, now Utah State paleontologist, who continues to direct the excavation.

The Morrison Formation holds more than dinosaur bones and stones. As Dr. Martin Lockley, professor at the University of Colorado in Denver, puts it, "A dinosaur only leaves one set of bones, but it can leave thousands of footprints."

There are dinosaur footprints or trackways almost everywhere. Just outside Denver, a short drive brings you to Dinosaur Ridge. Along this road, bones are visible. You can also see a slab of rock where it looks as though dinosaurs climbed straight up the mountain!

Ancient tracks have a special appeal. What we're looking at is the record from the remote past of a living animal in action. Dinosaur tracks turn up worldwide and not just from the Jurassic period.

Imagine a 30-ton brontosaur walking along the shoreline of a lake. The ground is soft. Its feet sink a little into the mud. Each foot leaves a depression, just as your feet do when you walk along a beach. Now imagine the prints exposed to the sun; the ground dries up and hardens. A light breeze blows along the shore, and the sand of a nearby dune slowly fills the tracks of our brontosaur. Over time, more layers of sediment accumulate and turn to rock, but the tracks are still there,

Why did the dinosaurs disappear?

There may not be a single simple answer. One theory suggests that volcanic activity was responsible. Large volcanic eruptions did take place at about the time of dinosaur extinction. Ash could have darkened the sky, while gases such as carbon dioxide would have ultimately triggered acid rain, killing the vegetation and many animals.

WERE ALL FIERCE MEAT-EATING DINOSAURS HUGE?

Many were. But one of the most efficient was rather small. Called Deinonychus, it weighed about 100 pounds and was eight feet long. It had the tools to bring down big prey: speed, brains, the ability to hunt in packs, and sharp claws and teeth.

invisible. Millions of years later, these rocks erode. Layer after layer peels off, until the one carrying the brontosaur tracks is exposed to our view.

Over the 165 million years of dinosaur history, countless tracks have been preserved. These trackways tell fascinating stories.

For instance, near Tuba City, Arizona, you can see theropod tracks of the first big meat-eating dinosaurs on a surface of red sandstone. Most are nearly a foot long. One special track, however, measures a few inches. Was it a small adult or a juvenile? Was it alone or following an adult? We don't know.

Farther east, the state of Connecticut has its own Dinosaur State Park, where hundreds of theropod footprints are now exposed and preserved for you to see.

In eastern Colorado, where Dr. Lockley has studied and mapped for many years, there is a site where many brontosaurs followed an ancient shoreline. Some of these brontosaurs were only half-grown. They traveled in groups. In one spot, five parallel trackways are clearly visible. Nearby, a much bigger brontosaur ventured out into too-soft ground, and his feet sank two or three feet into the mud.

Meat-eating theropods were present too, hunters and scavengers looking for a meal or coming to the lake to drink. They left their

three-toed birdlike footprints. These tracks did not happen all at once on a particular day. The gray mudstone carrying the tracks has many layers on top of one another. Each layer shows its own set of tracks. This particular lake existed for thousands of years, and dinosaurs of many generations came and went and came back again.

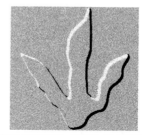

CRETACEOUS: time runs out

At the end of the Jurassic, 144 million years ago, we see a major change in both the animal fossils and the type of sediments. Why and how do such changes take place? There is no simple answer. The position of the continents and the rise and fall of sea levels make major impacts on climate. It's possible that communities of Jurassic plants and animals, well-adapted to a certain environment and climate, became imbalanced at some point and could not adapt to new conditions.

Whatever the reasons, something happened at the end of the Jurassic. By the middle of the Cretaceous, the glory days of the sauropods came to an end. A few hung on in North America and other parts of the world, but nothing like the splendor of Jurassic times.

We know little about the beginnings of this new epoch, because few rocks were deposited in North America. For the first 25 million years of the Cretaceous, paleontologists have to look to other sites such as Europe. In England, some *Diplodocus*-like sauropods survived and left fossils. Most importantly, a different sort of animal became

Dinosaur Imagery ©1993 Dinamation International Corporation

widespread: the ornithopods. Among them was the *Iguanodon,* the famous bipedal dinosaur described by 19th-century naturalists.

As we move forward in time, the fossil record improves. Bones and many footprints of early Cretaceous dinosaurs are found in Southern Texas, at that time a warm habitat of lowlands and shallow lagoons.

HOW DO WE KNOW DINOSAURS LAID EGGS?
Because their eggs have come to light in many parts of the world. Top photo: part of a clutch of fossil eggs, each 5 inches in diameter, found in Henan Province in China. Bottom photo: a computer-animated model of eggs and hatchlings in the nest of a *Parasaurolophus,* a type of hadrosaur. Paleontologists believe some dinosaurs nested in colonies, just as penguins do today.

21

Near Glen Rose, Texas, a famous trackway can be seen in the limestone beneath the muddy waters of the Paluxy River at Dinosaur Valley State Park. It combines large prints of plant-eating sauropods with smaller ones from their predators. Some people have examined the imperfect footprints of this small, bird-hipped, meat-eating dinosaur and misinterpreted them as the tracks of human beings. A few people have even pointed to these prints as 'proof' that dinosaurs and humans once co-existed.

We might daydream that humans and dinosaurs once lived together. But when these dinosaurs walked along the shores of the warm ancestral Gulf of Mexico, anything looking like a human being was still 100 million years in the future.

Two important dinosaurs show up in the early to mid-Cretaceous years. One is *Deinonychus* or 'terrible claw,' discovered and described by John Ostrom of Yale University. It lived in Montana and other parts of the American West. *Utahraptor* is the other important dinosaur which lived earlier in this era.

A formidable predator, *Deinonychus* walked on two legs, had a long snout armed with razor–sharp teeth, plus well-developed arms and hands equipped with claws with which to grasp its prey. The animal also possessed long and sharp sicklelike claws on the second toe of each foot, with which it could disembowel its victims. Its tail vertebrae were surrounded by numerous bony tendons. These must have made the tail as stiff as a balancing pole. The picture we get is of an active, agile, and fast animal. It could run on its two legs, the tail balancing the weight of the head and torso. 'Terrible claw' could jump on its prey, grasp it, and use its sickle claw to deliver rapid fatal blows.

This hunter and others like it led John Ostrom to speculate that in order to be so active, these dinosaurs must have had high body temperatures. This notion began an important debate: were any of the dinosaurs warm-blooded?

With the help of his *Deinonychus,* John Ostrom also took another look at the origin of the birds puzzle.

At the British Museum of Natural History, under lock and key, is an *Archaeopteryx* – the first known bird. This fossil has been described as the most valuable of all fossils. It lived in Jurassic times – that is, before *Deinonychus.*

Archaeopteryx turned up in 1861 in the lithographic limestone quarries in Bavaria. Its fossil even shows its feathers and teeth, delicately preserved in the fine-grained rocks that artists used to reproduce and print their drawings.

23

Centrosaurus

Centrosaurus was a powerful ceratopsid, with a single horn
born on its nose. It may have lived in herds for protection.
Albertosaurus probably did not kill large herds of dinosaurs
very often but would scavenge the carcasses of those that
perished from other causes.

Centrosaurus

Nineteenth-century scientists recognized *Archaeopteryx* as a link between reptiles and birds, with special features found only in dinosaurs. Sir Richard Owen, who named the Dinosauria, Thomas Henry Huxley, who championed Darwin's theory of evolution, and Othniel Marsh, the American dinosaur expert, all accepted the idea.

In the early 20th century, however, a new generation of researchers questioned *Archaeopteryx's* direct link to the dinosaurs. Some thought there might be an even more ancient common ancestor to birds and dinosaurs.

With the discovery of *Deinonychus,* John Ostrom found evidence that he thought could change that point of view again. He began to show that birds evolved from some active little theropod very much like the *Deinonychus* of the early Cretaceous.

The hands and hips of *Deinonychus* and *Archaeopteryx* are very similar, in spite of the size difference and the geological time that separates them. It may be that a small theropod, the common ancestor of both *Deinonychus* and *Archaeopteryx,* still lies buried in some Jurassic rock, awaiting discovery.

The fossil record of birds is incomplete. *Archaeopteryx* is the first true bird we've found, and as such it is invaluable.

The birds, an entirely new group of creatures, followed their own path of evolution. They developed feathers, which are modified reptile scales. Their feathers insulated them well. They allowed birds to glide between branches and trees and eventually to fly. The rest of the dinosaur world remained on the ground, continuing to evolve into a whole range of new species.

Bird fossils show up again in the chalk deposits of Kansas of the late Cretaceous. By now, they look much more like modern birds. One of them, *Ichthyornis,* resembled a tern. It probably flew over lagoons and shallow seas to catch fish. The other, *Hesperornis,* was a good swimmer and more like a flightless loon. Both species still had teeth.

Eventually, before the final extinction of the dinosaurs, true modern birds appeared, having lost their teeth. These birds left their footprints in the soft sediments of lakes and rivers. They evolved and changed up to the present day, where they are one of the most successful branches of the animal kingdom. There are more than 8,500 different species of birds now. Are they evolutionary descendants of the dinosaurs? John Ostrom and many others think so.

In 1991, an animal belonging to the same family as *Deinonychus* turned up in Utah. Dr. Jim Kirkland and Don Burge, College of Eastern Utah Prehistoric Museum Director, were its discoverers. Kirkland named it *Utahraptor* – the Utah thief. It lived before *Deinonychus.*

SINCE DINOSAURS ARE EXTINCT, HOW CAN WE KNOW HOW THEY LOOKED AND ACTED? In the last 150 years, scientists have learned much about them. Museums and science centers now have displays that take you right into this long-ago world. For example, this display at the Canadian Royal Tyrrell Museum shows an *Albertosaurus* making a meal of a *Centrosaurus.* The best museums use lighting, videos, skeletons, moving models, dioramas of the creatures in their habitats, and many other elements to make dinosaur life come alive.

Deinonychus stood about four feet. *Utahraptor* towered nine feet! *Utahraptor* had long sicklelike claws on its second toes. At 1,000 pounds, it must have been a terrifying hunter. Even a large sauropod would have been in danger from it. As thought for *Deinonychus,* it's possible that *Utahraptor* lived and hunted in packs. When they lived, these animals were the most intelligent creatures on earth.

During Cretaceous times, the geography of North America slowly changed. In the middle of the continent, a depression formed. The sea level also rose globally. Shallow seas moved toward one another from the north and south. Eventually, the continents of Asia, Africa, and North America were divided by water. From the Gulf of Mexico to the Arctic, a sea covered the present-day plains states of the Midwest.

Along the western shores through the area that is now Colorado and New Mexico, thousands of *Iguanodon*-like dinosaurs left millions of footprints, best seen at Dinosaur Ridge near Denver. Because this shoreline, possibly an ancient migration route, is trampled for thousands of square miles, paleontologists call it 'the Dinosaur Freeway.'

Between this ancient sea and the Rocky Mountains, where much volcanic activity was going on, a long and narrow plain formed.

We know a great deal about the dinosaur communities living on that long-ago plain. Their fossils are well exposed in Montana, Canada, and along the entire western margin of the seaway south into Mexico.

Many paleontologists think that life on that plain was similar to the mammal communities we see today on the Serengeti Plain of East Africa. On it, large groups of duckbill dinosaurs moved about. Herds of horned dinosaurs, *Triceratops* among them, foraged along the rivers, browsing the shrubs. There were armored dinosaurs, protected by bony plates on their backs and spikes all around. There were ostrichlike dinosaurs that caught lizards with their toothless beaks. Small theropods hunted for their meals. The largest meat-eater, the fearsome *Tyrannosaurus rex,* harried the herds, occasionally attacking the isolated duckbill.

The herbivorous armies of dinosaurs were feeding on something relatively new: flowering plants, today's most common and abundant species. In Jurassic times, flowers didn't exist. They appeared at the beginning of the Cretaceous.

Dr. Robert Bakker has suggested that dinosaurs and flowering plants co-evolved. As he puts it, "Dinosaurs invented flowers."

Why did the dinosaurs disappear?

There may not be a single simple answer.
Above the K-T boundary – the white line in this
photo – no dinosaurs are found.
This thin geologic layer
contains up to 30 times more iridium
than the surrounding rocks.
Did this rare mineral come from deep within
the earth, ejected by volcanoes?
Or from a space object, such as
a giant asteroid?

Plants protect themselves from competing plants and from being eaten by all sorts of chemical and mechanical adaptations. Confronted with large herds of hungry dinosaurs, the plants that could tolerate grazing best and could reproduce and grow the fastest – those using flowers and pollination – had an advantage. So in late Cretaceous times, flowering plants came to dominate the landscape.

At the same time these events were happening on the plains of North America, the tiny *Velociraptor* – the cunning, speedy predator of "Jurassic Park" book fame – came into its own in the arid desert terrain of China and Mongolia. (The *'Velociraptor'* in the movie "Jurassic Park" more resembled an oversized *Deinonychus*.)

PALEONTOLOGIST & GEOLOGIST

Dr. James Kirkland
works with care to uncover
a *Utahraptor* skeleton,
the ferocious hunter
he discovered in conjunction
with the College of Eastern Utah
Prehistoric Museum.
At right, in his hands,
is a cast of the 9-inch core
of a *Utahraptor* claw.

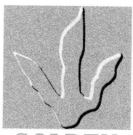

n this, the Golden Age of dinosaur discovery, new slices of past life continue to amaze us.

One such story is the discovery of the nesting duck-billed dinosaurs. That dinosaurs produced eggs was known and expected. After all, most reptiles and all birds do. The first dinosaur eggs were found in France but little could be learned from them. Why? Because the remains of the parent dinosaurs were not found.

In the 1920s, the American Museum of Natural History of New York sent a series of expeditions to the Gobi Desert in Asia. Its leader, Roy Chapman Andrews, gained popular and scientific fame by discovering the first dinosaur nests, complete with eggs. He attributed them to *Protoceratops,* a small horned dinosaur, common in the late Cretaceous of Mongolia.

Little was known about the nesting behavior of dinosaurs until 1979, when American paleontologist John Horner and his friend

Bob Makela, led by clues from a rock shop, dug in the Montana earth and discovered the nesting grounds of a large species of duckbill, as well as a smaller animal.

This duckbill belonged to a new species. Horner and Makela named it *Maiasaura,* or 'good mother lizard.' The adult animals were 20- to 25-feet long. For the first time, John Horner proved that dinosaurs cared for their offspring.

The nests he found measured about six feet in diameter, surrounded by a rim about three-feet tall. In one of the nests lay the remains of 15 baby dinosaurs. They had

died there – perhaps because their parents could not return to feed and take care of them. The eggshells were trampled and broken. The bones of the babies were not grown to the point where the young animals could have traveled away from the nest on their own. Horner found debris and vegetation in the nest, which may have been part of the food the parents had been bringing to the babies.

ver several years, Horner and crew found more nests, forming a loosely arranged colony. The distance between nests was about equal to the length of an adult animal.

Nowadays, there are not many animals which nest in colonies. Birds do, especially sea birds, flamingos, and pelicans. In these colonies, the distance between nests is more or less the length of an adult bird. Why? Because the territory one bird sitting on its nest can defend corresponds to the distance its beak can reach to strike an intruder. The way the duck-billed dinosaurs nested reminds us of modern birds.

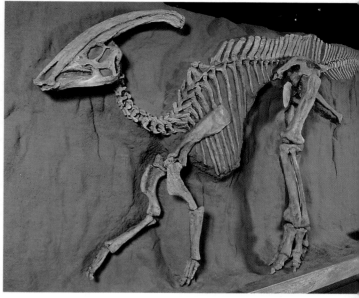

Other details emerged. The nests of a colony of hypsilophodontids, a small two-legged dinosaur, were found in several successive layers of rocks. This indicated that the dinosaurs came back to the same nesting site. This is another birdlike behavior.

Horner was also surprised to find a huge bone bed, estimated to contain the remains of a herd of some 10,000 duckbills. None of the skeletons were complete. The bones were scattered and mixed, showing they were moved some distance after the death of the animals, perhaps by a river in flood. All of these dinosaurs probably died together, most likely poisoned by gases during a volcanic eruption.

How could such huge herds of large animals find enough food in one area? They couldn't for long. They had to keep moving. Like today's wildebeests of the Serengeti, they must have had to migrate, following the cycle of the rains and the growth of the vegetation.

Some dinosaur herds migrated clear to Alaska, where the climate was warmer than it is today, and the North Slope was a coastal plain. Trees could grow there and sustain a large population of herbivores. Most likely, the dinosaurs did not stay up north during the winter.

Can traditional cold-blooded reptiles migrate long distances? The only ones to do so are the sea turtles.

The discovery that large herds of dinosaurs migrated makes it more likely that these animals had a metabolism different than the reptilian one. So we are back to the issue of warm-bloodedness, the question raised by John Ostrom and his work on active theropods. Many paleontologists are now convinced that dinosaurs – at least some species – were warm-blooded.

WHAT DID THE HADROSAURS, POPULARLY CALLED DUCK-BILLED DINOSAURS, LOOK LIKE?
In the Cretaceous period, they were a very successful group of plant eaters. They moved in herds. Some nested in colonies and cared for their babies. Several species developed crests on top of their heads. Parasaurolophus, pictured on these pages, had a huge crest. The skeleton at right shows its broad beak and long low skull. In their jaws, they had up to 1,200 teeth.

A 'DINOSAUR FREEWAY'

How do we know that some dinosaurs moved in herds? Through the discovery and study of much-used trackways nicknamed 'dinosaur freeways.' Author and Professor of Geology Dr. Martin Lockley, who has studied dinosaur tracks on several continents, is pictured with one of his discoveries. Fossil footprints give clues to herding habits, social organization, migration, and other aspects of dinosaur behavior. This place, where five enormous Apatosaurus or Brontosaurus tracks wander side by side, is located at the Purgatoire site in the Morrison Formation.

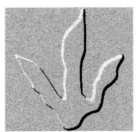

MYSTERY of the K-T Boundary

The dinosaurs vanished. All we have are the birds, our unlikely looking link with them. About the same time the great marine reptiles and many other animals disappeared, so did the dinosaurs. The questions are: why and when?

The date of extinction has often been answered with a simple number: 65 million years ago. But is that true? Or rather, can the timing of extinction be pinpointed with this kind of accuracy? A single event? Some scientists think so. Others don't.

All around the world, there exists a layer in the earth, a geological formation you can touch, put your finger on, and say: below this line there were dinosaurs on the land. Above it, no more. This line is called the K-T boundary. "K" is an abbreviation for Cretaceous. "T" stands for Tertiary, the geological period that follows the Cretaceous.

The K-T line is a fine layer of clay, usually less than one inch thick. It has a high content of a rare mineral not normally found on the surface of the earth: iridium. This element, similar to platinum, exists deep in the mantle of our planet. It's also found in space objects, such as asteroids.

Why did the dinosaurs disappear?

There may not be a single simple answer.
An important theory, proposed in 1980
by a U.C. Berkeley team of scientists, says that a huge
asteroid hit the earth, creating a vast crater and a nuclear
winter. Dust rose, temperatures fell, and the world
was in darkness. This caused plants to die.
Eventually both plant-eating and meat-eating dinosaurs
died. Big craters made by asteroids do exist on earth,
such as Meteor Crater in Arizona.
The crater blamed for the 'nuclear winter' theory
is located on Mexico's Yucatan Peninsula.

WHAT DID APATOSAURUS (OUR OLD FRIEND BRONTOSAURUS) LOOK LIKE?
A creature of vast neck and tail, Apatosaurus moved its 75-foot-long body on sturdy legs. With skeleton at right is Brent Breithaupt, curator, U. of Wyoming Geological Museum in Laramie. All the sauropods, including Apatosaurus, had very small mouths for their size. This would seem a great handicap for an animal that had to eat as much as it did. In spite of this, they remained common for millions of years.

Dinosaur Imagery ©1993 Dinamation International Corporation

How did the K-T boundary get to be there? Was the material first spewed out by raging volcanoes? Or did an asteroid strike the planet, explode, and the vaporized contents, mixed with blasted rock and dust, fall steadily back to earth and get deposited into this iridium-rich layer? Even if one or both of these events happened 65 million years ago, did they wipe out the dinosaurs? Or were the dinosaurs on their way out already, for other reasons?

In 1980, U.C. Berkeley Nobel Prize-winning astrophysicist Luis Alvarez, his geologist son Walter, and their colleagues, discovered the abnormal nature of the deposit at the K-T boundary. They theorized that an asteroid six miles in diameter had struck the earth. When it hit, vast amounts of dust and other materials rose into the stratosphere and circled the globe, falling again slowly. This created a 'nuclear winter.' Temperatures dropped. Darkness reigned. Plants had no light, so photosynthesis stopped. The plant-eaters, such as many of the dinosaurs, were deprived of food. In time, so were the predators. All of the large animals died.

The impact of such a large asteroid must have left a crater. It took nearly ten years for geologists to recognize what they think is the evidence. The crater sits at the north end of the Yucatan Peninsula in Mexico. It's the right age and size. It's also the right position to help explain other phenomena associated with the K-T boundary. (One such oddity is the sea-bottom sediments that were washed over land as if by a tidal wave. They have been found in South Texas and Haiti.)

After 65 million years, the Yucatan crater is buried under a 2,000-foot-thick blanket of sediment. At the level of the crater, the rocks have been broken up by the explosion. But did it kill the dinosaurs?

The K-T boundary layer also contains what is called 'shocked quartz.' These are tiny grains of quartz fused in a way that can only happen during a powerful explosion. Some physicists say that quartz can fuse during volcanic eruptions. Did the asteroid impact trigger volcanic activity? Did it create the formation called the Deccan Traps, a place in India where a fissure poured out thousands of feet of lava?

There was a major impact that hit the earth at the end of the Cretaceous. The Deccan Traps do exist. They must have affected the earth's climate. But some researchers have shown that dinosaurs were declining long before the end of the Cretaceous. There were many individuals, but fewer species. The replacement rate of species had slowed.

WHAT DID STEGOSAURUS LOOK LIKE?

Almost everyone recognizes the bony plates
that run from its neck midway down its tail.
At the end of its tail, Stegosaurus wore four spikes,
which may have served as defense weapons.
The plates themselves may have been
for keeping cool – or warm.
This plant eater had one of the smallest
brains around – about the size of a walnut.

We need to remember that extinction of species is a normal process on earth. Species appear, become extinct, and are replaced by new ones. For example, we know that no dinosaur species lasted much more than five to ten million years, before evolving into a new species or going extinct. Scientists generally agree, however, that the last dinosaurs did not continue the normal process of extinction.

Dinosaurs fascinate us. The fact they disappeared is part of the fascination. Naturally enough, researchers continue to try to explain what happened to them. Recently, researchers measured air bubbles trapped in ancient amber. They found evidence that the oxygen content of air may have changed drastically back in time.

Or could it have been disease (carried by migrating species) that eliminated the dinosaurs, as Dr. Bakker has suggested?

Will we ever know what happened? The proof may be locked away somewhere, unrecognized as yet. Perhaps the mystery will never be solved to everyone's satisfaction. Perhaps you'll be the one to solve it!

Have you ever wanted to join a dinosaur dig? Besides the adventure, many dinosaur finds have been made by amateur paleontologists. In 1971, for example, Eddie and Vivian Jones found bones on Uncompahgre Plateau in Colorado. They called paleontologist Jim Jensen at Brigham Young University, who dug up *Ultrasaurus* and *Supersaurus* at the site.

No matter how enthusiastic an amateur paleontologist you become, the important thing is to work within the law. It's illegal to dig for dinosaur remains without a permit.

Since I've become interested in dinosaurs, I've had great fun working under the direction of professionals. I've worked on digs in Mexico, Argentina, and all around the American West. It's easy to join an organized expedition. Under professional supervision, kids are allowed to participate at certain digs in Colorado. They routinely find ribs, vertebrae, and allosaur teeth.

You may not make a career of paleontology. But if you're interested in dinosaurs, there's nothing like putting your hands into the earth and touching these mysterious old bones. As I've camped on the plains, listening to the stories told by the paleontologists, it seems to me that the dinosaurs have left much more than their bones for us to find.

VOLUNTEER
Connie Van Beek
brushes earth from the tailbones
of a huge *Diplodocus* found
near Sheep Creek, Wyoming.
A musician, Connie is one
of many amateur enthusiasts
who help support the work
of professional paleontology
by taking part in dinosaur digs.

WHAT DINOSAURS WORE

Every day we learn more about these ancient animals: how they moved, found food, defended themselves, took mates, and raised their young. In the process, we gain clues about how dinosaurs looked, how they saw each other, and how they adapted to their surroundings.

In our book, along with bones and tracks, you'll see numerous photos of life-size dinosaur models, most of them courtesy of Dinamation International Corporation, a company which builds reconstructions of dinosaurs for exhibits around the world. Much of our information in this section comes from the work their scientists and technical artisans have done in this area.

DINO VISION:

Dinosaurs probably saw in color. Their skulls show they had big eyes and a lot of brain space devoted to vision. Although they still possess many reptilian traits, their closest living relatives are the birds. Both reptiles and birds see in color. They're often brightly colored and patterned – another reason why we believe many dinosaur species wore colors or patterns.

DINO MOTION:

Not all dinosaurs were big, but those that were probably had heating and cooling problems. Animals with large body mass – such as elephants – use their big ears to regulate their body heat. The big plates you see on the back of a *Stegosaurus* may well have served the same purpose.

Dinosaurs also migrated. They lived in many different climates around the world. Some of their body ornaments – and their colors – would have been useful to keep warm or to keep cool.

Certain dinosaurs also carried weapons. The heavy tail club of the *Ankylosaurus,* a tank-sized plant eater, helped it protect itself. The horned neck frill and bony spines of the *Triceratops* on page 11 and the *Styracosaurus,* pictured on our cover, may have served the same purpose.

In the late Cretaceous, many dinosaur species had elaborate headdresses or body armor.
Page 42 is a nodosaur called Edmontonia;
page 43, right, is the skull of an Anchiceratops.
Page 43, left, is the skull of a Chasmosaurus.
All three are on display at the Royal Tyrrell Museum in Alberta, Canada.

DINO MUSIC:

At least two dinosaurs we know of had large hollow head crests, which were probably used for vocalizing. Breathing tubes run from the nostrils of the *Lambeosaurus* and the *Parasaurolophus* into their crests. In some species of *Lambeosaurus,* the crest is bigger than the skull. These dinosaurs may have been very musical. Or noisy!

DINO MATING:

In nature, reproduction is a big reason for animal ornamentation – things like peacocks' tails and mooses' antlers. Males often wear attention-getting horns, crests, fins, neck frills, and colors. They display to win the hearts of females and to bully other males. We don't know how often dinosaurs fought their rivals. One species named *Pachycephalosaurus* wore a cap of bone ten inches thick on its head. Perhaps it used its head as a battering ram, as bighorn sheep do today.

DINO DISGUISE:

Not all dinosaurs were fierce or large. Some needed to blend into the background or to look like other, fiercer creatures. Like tiger stripes or spots on a fawn, color patterns on dinosaur skin could have concealed creatures that didn't want to be discovered – or eaten. As the young of other species do, baby dinosaurs may have worn protective coloration.

ABOUT THE AUTHOR & PHOTOGRAPHER

This book stems from naturalist François Gohier's fascination with the large and majestic creatures of the earth. Author and photographer of three books on whales, François has spent 20 years documenting their lives and behaviors. His photos of animals large and small grace numerous books, calendars, posters, and magazines, such as *National Geographic, GEO,* and *Animal Kingdom.*

With this book, François set out to create a photographic record of dinosaurs that combines their physical remains and their human discoverers with memorable images of the best-imagined full-scale models. The results speak for themselves.

Illustrations throughout the book are imaginative interpretations of ferns, ginkgoes, and other plant foods that dinosaurs are thought to have dined on. They are the work of artist and book designer Ashala Nicols Lawler.

SPECIAL THANKS

For their kind contributions to manuscript and caption review, help with on-site photographic needs and permissions, and other liaison and assistance, the editors and the author sincerely wish to thank: Dr. George Callison, Sarah Morgan, Dr. Robert Bakker, Nick Liberato, and the Dinamation International Corporation; Dr. James Kirkland, Director Michael Perry, and the Dinamation International Society; Dr. Martin Lockley, Professor of Geology, University of Colorado; Dr. John Horner; Bob Farrar, the Black Hills Institute of Geological Research, Hill City, South Dakota; Dr. Phil Currie, Royal Tyrrell Museum of Paleontology, Alberta, Canada; Dinosaur Provincial Park, Alberta, Canada; Smith Studios, Bozeman, Montana; Curator Brent Breithaupt, University of Wyoming Geological Museum, Laramie, Wyoming; Dinosaur National Monument, Jensen, Utah; Don Burge, the College of Eastern Utah Prehistoric Museum, Price, Utah; the Patagonia Museum of Paleontology, Trelew, Argentina; Joni Hunt, Blake Books; Samantha Bradley, Silver Burdett.

OUTSTANDING PLACES TO SEE TRACKWAYS

♦ 'Dinosaur Freeway' and Dinosaur Ridge – near Denver, Colorado
♦ Purgatoire Valley tracksite – S.E. Colorado
♦ Dinosaur State Park – Rocky Hill, Connecticut
♦ Dinosaur Valley State Park – near Glen Rose, Texas
♦ Clayton Lake State Park – near Seneca, New Mexico

HANDS-ON DIGS, EXHIBITS, TOURS & MORE

♦ **Dinamation International Society.** Write D.I.S. at 550 Crossroads Court, Fruita, Colorado 81521, for info on this non-profit society: membership benefits; expeditions, tours, digs, and programs such as Family Dino Camp; exhibits and special programming at Devils Canyon Science & Learning Center.
♦ **Traveling exhibits:** Dinamation International Corporation makes animated, life-size, and realistic dinosaurs and other creatures which travel to 100+ museums, parks, and zoos throughout the world each year. Write D.I.C. Marketing Dept, 189-A Technology Drive, Irvine, California 92718 for exhibit locations and new Dinamation Centers.

DINO-SIGHTSEEING MUSTS

Part of the Morrison Formation is called **'the dinosaur triangle'** (Price, Utah – Vernal, Utah – Grand Junction, Colorado):
♦ Dinosaur National Monument – near Dinosaur, Colorado and Jensen, Utah
♦ Dinosaur Hill – near Grand Junction, Colorado
♦ Devils Canyon Science & Learning Center – Fruita, Colorado
♦ BYU Earth Science Museum – Provo, Utah
♦ Utah Museum of Natural History – Salt Lake City
♦ CEU Prehistoric Museum – Price, Utah

SOME OF THE BEST DINOSAUR MUSEUMS IN THE U.S.

♦ Academy of Natural Sciences – Philadelphia, Pennsylvania
♦ American Museum of Natural History – New York, New York
♦ California Academy of Science – San Francisco, California
♦ Carnegie Museum of Natural History – Pittsburgh, Pennsylvania
♦ Children's Museum of Indianapolis, Indiana
♦ Field Museum of Natural History – Chicago, Illinois
♦ Fort Worth Museum of Science and History – Ft. Worth, Texas
♦ Museum of Geology – Rapid City, South Dakota
♦ National Museum of Natural History – Washington, D.C.
♦ Natural History Museum of Los Angeles County, California
♦ New Mexico Museum of Natural History – Albuquerque, New Mexico
♦ Peabody Museum of Natural History – New Haven, Connecticut

165 Million Years of Dinosaurs: Resource Pages

MESOZOIC			CENOZOIC	P R E S E N T
Triassic	Jurassic	Cretaceous		

245   208   144   66

First Dinosaurs
about 230 million years ago

Last Dinosaurs
about 65 million years ago

First Modern Humans
1.5 million years ago

Graph not to scale. Source: *Decade of North American Geology – Geologic Time Scale*

MUSEUMS & SITES IN CANADA

- ◆ Calgary Zoo's Prehistoric Park – Calgary, Alberta
- ◆ Canadian Museum of Nature – Ottawa, Ontario
- ◆ Dinosaur Provincial Park – near Patricia, Alberta
- ◆ Museum of Natural Sciences – Saskatoon, Saskatchewan
- ◆ Royal Ontario Museum – Toronto, Ontario
- ◆ Royal Tyrrell Museum of Paleontology – Drumheller, Alberta

TEACHER RESOURCES

SOFTWARE & ONLINE SERVICES
- ◆ Learn About Dinosaurs (K-3) and Project Classify: Dinosaurs (gr. 3-6) from Sunburst/Wings for Learning, 101 Castleton St, Pleasantville, New York 10570 Call 800 321-7511 for catalog.
- ◆ Dinosaur Forum on CompuServe

FILMS & VIDEOS
- ◆ *Age of Dinosaurs* (4-film series, el-jr high: Troll 1988)
- ◆ *Digging Dinosaurs* (el-jr high: Centre Prod. 1988)
- ◆ *Dinosaurs!* (4 programs, all ages: Fox/Lorber 1991)
- ◆ *The Great Dinosaur Hunt* (Vestron Video 1989)
- ◆ *Where Did They Go? A Dinosaur Update* (el-jr high: Rainbow Educational Video 1988)

BOOKS
- ◆ *Digging Dinosaurs*, J. Horner & J. Gorman (Workman 1988)
- ◆ *Dinosaur Heresies*, R. Bakker (Morrow 1986)
- ◆ *Tracking Dinosaurs*, M. Lockley (Cambridge U. Press 1989)
- ◆ *New Illustrated Dinosaur Dictionary* (Lothrop 1994)
- ◆ *Dinosaur Safari Guide*, V. Costa (Voyageur Press 1994). This well-written, map-filled guide describes 170+ dinosaur sites and exhibits in the U.S. and Canada; recommended for the whole family.

CAST OF CHARACTERS

Albertosaurus (al-BURT-oh-sore-us) – lizard from Alberta 24-25
Allosaurus (Al-o-SORE-us) – leaping lizard 7, 12, 17, 22-23
Anchiceratops (ANK-ee-SARE-uh-tops) – close-horned face 43
Ankylosaurus (an-KYLE-o-SORE-us) – stiffened lizard 10, 42
Apatosaurus/aka Brontosaurus – (a-PAT-o-SORE-us/ BRAHN-toe-SORE-us) – deceptive lizard/thunder lizard 8, 12, 16, 17, 23, 32-33, 36, 37
Archaeopteryx (ark-e-OP-ter-icks) – ancient wing 23, 25
Brachiosaurus (BRAK-ee-o-SORE-us) – arm lizard 8
Camarasaurus (cam-ARE-a-SORE-us) – chambered lizard 16, 17
Centrosaurus (SENT-roe-sore-us) – pointed lizard 24-25
ceratopsids (SARE-a-TOP-sids) – horned-faced lizard 10
Chasmosaurus (KAZ-moe-sore-us) – gaping lizard 43
coelurosaur (seel-YOUR-oh-sore) – hollow-tailed lizard 17
Deinonychus (die-NAH-nick-us) – terrible claw 20, 22, 23, 25, 26, 27
Diplodocus (dip-LAH-duh-kus) – double beam 8, 12, 17, 21, 41
Edmontonia (ED-mon-TONE-ee-yah) – from Edmonton 42
Eoraptor (EE-o-RAP-tor) – early thief 12
hadrosaurs (HAD-row-sores) – duck-billed lizards 2, 8-10, 21, 26, 31
Herrerasaurus (her-RARE-uh-SORE-us) – Herrera's lizard 12
Hesperornis (HES-per-ORN-iss) – western bird 25
hypsilophodontids (HYPE-sel-O-foe-DON-tids) – high-ridged teeth 10, 31
Ichthyornis (IK-thee-ORN-iss) – fish bird 25
ichthyosaurs (IK-thee-o-SORES) – fish lizards 7
Iguanodon (ig-WAN-o-don) – iguana-tooth 4, 10, 17, 21, 26
Kritosaurus (KRIT-oh-sore-us) – chosen lizard 46
Lambeosaurus (LAM-bee-oh-sore-us) – Lambe's lizard 43
Maiasaura (MY-uh-sore-uh) – good-mother lizard 29
nodosaurs (NO-doe-sores) – knobby, bumpy lizards 10, 42
ornithischians (orn-ith-ISS-key-yans) – bird-hipped 7, 8, 10
Pachycephalosaurus (PAK-ee-seff-uh-low-SORE-us) – thick-headed lizard 10, 43
Parasaurolophus (pair-uh-sore-ALL-uh-fuss) – another crested lizard 20, 30, 31, 43
Pentaceratops (pent-uh-SARE-uh-tops) – five-horned face 10
Pisanosaurus (pi-ZAN-a-SORE-us) – Pisano's lizard 12
plesiosaurs (PLEE-zee-o-SORES) – near lizards 7
Protoceratops (PRO-toe-SARE-a-tops) – first horned face 29
Pteranodon (tare-RAN-o-don) – winged and toothless 7
saurischian (sore-ISS-key-yan) – lizard-hipped 7, 8
sauropods (SORE-o-PODS) – lizard-footed 1, 8, 15-18, 21, 22, 26, 36
Seismosaurus (SIZE-moe-SORE-us) – earth-shaking lizard 8, 18
Stegosaurus (STEG-o-SORE-us) – plated lizard 10, 12, 17, 38-39, 42
Styracosaurus (sty-RAK-oh-sore-us) – spiky lizard front cover, 42
Supersaurus (SOO-per-SORE-us) – super lizard 8, 40
theropods (THARE-o-pods) – wild beast foot 1, 8, 20, 25, 26, 31
Triceratops (try-SARE-a-tops) – three-horned faced 10-11, 26, 42
Tyrannosaurus rex (tie-RAN-o-SORE-us reks) – tyrant lizard king 2-3, 4-8, 26
Ultrasaurus (UL-truh-SORE-us) – ultra lizard 8, 40
Utahraptor (YOU-tah-RAP-tor) – Utah thief 22, 25, 26, 28, 29
Velociraptor (ve-LOS–e-RAP-tor) – fast thief 7, 27

"*If you love dinosaurs, there's nothing like putting your hands into the earth and touching these mysterious old bones...*"

François Gohier, author

Kritosaurus from Patagonia Museum of Paleontology, Trelew, Chubut, Argentina